The Power of Preparation
Set Yourself Up for Negotiation Success

Louis P. Wright

Table of Contents

The most important trip you may take in life is meeting people halfway.

— Henry Boye

Chapter 1. Introduction

Unleash the potential behind every conversation with our riveting Special Report: "The Power of Preparation: Set Yourself Up for Negotiation Success." Dive into the enigmatic world of negotiation, shattering the myth that it's a skill only for diplomats or business tycoons. In this approachable, joyfully engaging report, we unravel the essential tactics, strategies and maneuvers that can transform your negotiation outcomes. Don't fret if you're not a seasoned bargainer, because this report is all about equipping you with confidence, clarity, and control before you even set foot in the negotiation space. Bursting with lively anecdotes, practical exercises, and insightful advice, this report will empower you to take charge of any negotiation scenario. So why wait? Step into a realm where every conversation can turn into a triumph, and let this exciting journey bring out your inner negotiation Maestro!

Chapter 2. Understanding the Art of Negotiation

The art of negotiation is much more than the simple exchange of proposals and counterproposals, of concessions and compromises. It's a complex, fascinating tapestry of psychology, strategy, communication, and power dynamics, each woven delicately with the potential to shape the outcome of a negotiation in profound and unexpected ways. Like any form of art, it's subtle, nuanced, and deeply individualistic in its expression, subject to personal style, skill, and savvy.

2.1. Human behavior and Negotiation

Understanding the bedrock of negotiation begins with understanding human behavior. Negotiators aren't disembodied entities who engage in purely rational decision-making; they are humans, teeming with emotions, biases and aspirations. They bring their hopes, fears, vulnerabilities, and strengths to the negotiation table, subtly shaping the ebb and flow of the negotiation discourse. It helps to possess empathy and social insight - components of emotional intelligence - enabling one to read between lines, discern unmet needs or anticipate potential objections.

It's essential to acknowledge that negotiation is not about 'winning'. Real maturity in negotiation comes from appreciating that it's a problem-solving exercise, where the aim is not to triumph over rather work alongside the other party to create mutual value. A zero-sum mentality, where one's gain is necessarily the other's loss, is discouraged as it fosters hostility and defensive maneuvering, souring relationships and prospects for future negotiation.

2.2. Negotiation Styles and Strategies

Despite the unique flair that different negotiators bring, it's possible to distill certain common styles or approaches that negotiators adopt. At a rudimentary level, we find competitive negotiators and cooperative negotiators.

Competitive negotiators are assertive and uncompromising. They are primarily self-interested and are willing to use various pressure tactics to maximize their own outcomes. Generally, they make high demands and give few or measured concessions. But there's a risk involved: it may lead to an impasse when dealing with another competitive negotiator or damage ties in the long run.

Cooperative negotiators, on the other hand, demonstrate a more accommodating, relationship-oriented style. They lean toward problem-solving and collaboration. They are often more willing to make concessions for the sake of maintaining a congenial, lasting relationship with the other party. While such an approach can engender trust, it can also leave room for exploitation if not complemented by firmness and acuity.

The real art in negotiation is in finding the right balance between these polar approaches, in adjusting one's style to the nature of the relationship and the context of the negotiation.

2.3. Power Dynamics in Negotiations

Power dynamics play an integral role in negotiations. Power can stem from various sources - information, authority, skills, resources, or even personal attributes like charisma or articulation. It can be explicit or subtle, consistent or fluctuating. What matters is how one wields it, how one allows it to influence one's behavior, and how one responds to it.

Despite its importance, power does not assure success. An acute negotiator knows that unwarranted assertion of power can lead to deadlock and misunderstanding, while judiciously modulated power can create win-win situations. The power is not necessarily in the hands of the one who possesses more resources; it often lies in the hands of the one who cares the least about the outcome. Therefore, investments in alternative options, also known as BATNAs (Best Alternatives To a Negotiated Agreement), can limit one's dependence on the negotiation outcome and help balance power asymmetries.

2.4. Preparing for Negotiations

The path to negotiation success is paved with preparation. A good negotiator is not an improviser; she's a meticulous planner. Before entering any negotiation, understanding one's own and the other party's needs, constraints, and interests is vital. Understanding the bigger picture, the context in which the negotiation is happening, is equally important.

The key is to invest time in research. Explore all available information about the counterpart's past behavior, negotiation patterns, business profile, or any other relevant facets that might shed light on their negotiation approach, potential concessions, or red lines. Equally important is to self-audit - what are your motives and what constitutes a 'win' for you? What are your bottom lines? What are you willing or not willing to compromise on? Preparation reduces uncertainty and induces confidence, enhancing the likelihood of favorable outcomes.

Lastly, the most beautiful, most understated part of the art of negotiation is, perhaps, its potential for transformation. Done right, negotiation has the power to not only resolve conflicts but build bridges, foster understanding, and cultivate enduring partnerships. As you delve deeper into this art, you'll begin to appreciate its capacity for creating value, promoting dialogue, nurturing relationships, and catalyzing positive change in your personal, professional, and social lives. After all, like all art forms, the rewards of mastering negotiation reach far beyond its immediate canvas—it's a life skill. One that promises enriched connections, mutual growth, and more harmonious coexistence.

Chapter 3. Key Elements of Successful Negotiation

This chapter plunges into the heart of negotiation – the key elements that form the backbone of successful negotiation. Appreciating these elements and their interlinking dynamics is pivotal for a proficient negotiator. An understanding of what makes an effective negotiation will enable you to make sound decisions, foster productive relationships, and ultimately emerge triumphant in negotiation scenarios.

3.1. The Foundation: Preparation

Negotiation success owes much to laborious and strategic preparation. A successful negotiation isn't just measured by the final outcome, but also by how well-prepared you were for it. Gather information about the other party, anticipate their arguments, consider possible counter-arguments, and formulate a strategy. Core areas of preparation can be bucketed under understanding the negotiation context, knowing your counterpart, and having clarity on your interests and limits.

A defining aspect of preparation is cultivating a negotiation strategy. Weigh in on your strengths, weaknesses, opportunities and threats (also known as a SWOT analysis); draft plausible best-case, worst-case and likely-case scenarios; and frame a negotiation agenda that outlines the key points to be discussed.

3.2. Developing Mutual Trust and Understanding

Trust is the cornerstone of any negotiation process. It helps in constructive dialogue, encourages the sharing of information and fosters a collaborative atmosphere. Developing mutual trust may begin far in advance of the negotiation itself – through pre-existing relationships or preliminary meetings.

Understanding the needs, aspirations and constraints of your negotiation counterpart can help you create strategies that are not just about winning, but are also aimed at achieving acceptable outcomes for both parties. Displaying empathy and understanding towards your counterpart's perspectives paves the way for trust building and positive rapport.

3.3. Communication: Clear, Concise and Considerate

Communication forms an indispensable part of negotiation. Effective communicators are those who can portray their demands and necessities in a clear and concise manner, without appearing overbearing or confrontational. They can persuasively put forth their arguments while keeping room for feedback and suggestions.

Moreover, effective communication is as much about listening as it is about speaking. Good negotiators are active listeners, ever attentive to their counterpart's words, reading between the lines and picking up on subtle cues. Additionally, non-verbal communication, such as body language and facial expressions, can offer a wealth of information about the other party's thought processes and emotional state.

3.4. The Balance of Power

Understanding the power dynamics at play in any negotiation scenario is fundamental. Power in negotiation can stem from a plethora of sources – access to information, positional authority, personal influence, or even the ability to withstand losses better. Recognizing the magnitude and source of your own power, as well as that of your negotiation counterpart, can guide your negotiation strategy and tactics.

However, it's essential to wield your power in a manner that does not belittle or threaten the other party. Power should be used responsibly to promote constructive dialogue and to work towards mutually beneficial solutions.

3.5. The Art of Offering and Making Concessions

Negotiation invariably involves making and receiving concessions. The art lies in how skillfully you make offers that are favorable to you while simultaneously appealing to the other party. A concession is a give-and-take dynamic – it's pivotal to maintain a keen sense of balance, ensuring you don't give away too much too soon or hold back excessively.

3.6. The Closure: Agreement and Implementation

Reaching the finish line of a negotiation process involves finalizing an agreement and planning its implementation. Successful negotiators understand the need to craft agreements that are clear, detailed, and actionable, leaving no room for ambiguity or interpretation. After all, a successful negotiation isn't purely about reaching an agreement – it also involves ensuring that the agreement is effectively implemented and monitored.

The art of negotiation is multifaceted, shaped by an assortment of key elements. Mastery over these elements – preparation, mutual trust and understanding, effective communication, balance of power, skill in concession dynamics, and securing appropriate agreement and implementation – can guide you towards becoming a successful negotiator.

Chapter 4. The Psychology Behind Negotiation

In the realm of negotiation, appreciating the psychological underpinnings is akin to uncovering a secret language. This can help to predict and influence behaviors in negotiation scenarios. Armed with this insight, we can purposefully steer conversations to achieve desired outcomes.

4.1. Understanding Human Behavior

To comprehend the role psychology plays in negotiation, it's important to first understand fundamental human behavior. Psychological theories such as Maslow's Hierarchy of Needs, the Theory of Cognitive Dissonance, and the Social Identity Theory provide a solid foundation. Let's explore them.

4.2. Maslow's Hierarchy of Needs and Negotiation

In his iconic theory, psychologist Abraham Maslow suggested human motivation is driven by a series of needs ranging from very basic (physiological needs), to higher level (self-actualization). In the context of negotiation, fully cognizant negotiators can motivate their negotiation counterparts by tapping into these needs.

For instance, a skilled negotiator knows that directly appealing to a business need (safety need, in Maslow's terms) may be more persuasive than a purely monetary argument (physiological need). By showing how the proposed solution meets the business's security or stability needs, they increase the chances of negotiations progressing positively.

4.3. Theory of Cognitive Dissonance and Its Role

The Theory of Cognitive Dissonance posits that individuals strive for consistency and continuity in their beliefs and actions, and when they encounter opposing ideas, discomfort is generated. This discomfort, or dissonance, could be manipulated in negotiation scenarios to influence the opposition.

For example, if a negotiator confronts a company's representative with the fact that their current practices contradict their proclaimed environmental commitment (thus creating cognitive dissonance), the representative might be more likely to agree with a proposal that realigns the company's actions with its values.

4.4. Social Identity Theory in Negotiation

Social Identity Theory argues that individuals derive part of their sense of self from the groups they identify with. Recognizing the implications of this theory can prove beneficial for a negotiation setting.

If a negotiator can draw a correlation between the successful resolution of negotiations and a positive impact on a group or community that the other party values, the likelihood of gaining agreement increases.

4.5. The Role of Emotions

Emotions are inherent to the human experience and, therefore, inevitably make their way into the negotiation table. Through understanding the complex role emotions play, one can craft strategies that harness their power.

4.6. Emotions as Decision Drivers

Whilst it is commonly assumed that the best decisions are rational and devoid of emotion, a growing body of research suggests the opposite. Emotional reactions often drive people's decisions, including negotiation stances. Harnessing your own emotions, and being sensitive to the emotions of your negotiation counterpart, can significantly influence the negotiation process and its outcome.

4.7. The Importance of Emotional Intelligence

Understanding the emotional climate can be navigated with emotional intelligence – the ability to perceive, control, and evaluate emotions. Evidence shows that negotiators with high emotional intelligence tend to enjoy more positive interpersonal relationships and achieve better outcomes. They can empathize with their counterpart, anticipate emotional responses, and react appropriately, thus becoming effective influencers of the negotiation process.

4.8. The Emotional Tactical Maneuver

Skilled negotiators use emotional information as part of their tactics for effective negotiation. By understanding the other party's emotions, they can forecast responses and plan tactics. For instance, if the opposing negotiator appears to be nervous or unsure, it might be optimal to suggest a mutually beneficial trade-off to provide them with a sense of security.

4.9. Cognitive Biases in Negotiation

Our brains, while remarkable, are prone to errors due to cognitive biases. They distort our judgement, pushing us to make suboptimal decisions. Acknowledging these biases can help improve decision-making in negotiations.

4.10. Anchoring Bias

Anchoring bias is when individuals rely too heavily on the first piece of information they receive (the "anchor") when making decisions. To exploit this behavior in negotiations, you could consciously set the anchor point according to your preferred terms.

4.11. Confirmation Bias

Confirmation bias is the tendency to search for, interpret, favor, and recall information in a way that confirms one's pre-existing beliefs. By presenting arguments or evidence that supports the other party's initial viewpoint, a negotiator can build trust and steer negotiations favorably.

4.12. Availability Heuristic

The availability heuristic is a decision-making shortcut that relies on immediate examples that come to mind. In negotiation, should a negotiator be aware of this bias, they can bring convincing examples and analogies to help shape the narrative in their favor.

Living through each negotiation scenario from a psychological perspective allows us to recognize behavioral patterns, then use or counteract them as needed. This analysis of negotiation psychology provides a comprehensive view into the profound and complex dimensions of human behavior influencing negotiation outcomes. It does not merely rely on the mechanics of negotiating tactics. Instead, it dives deep into the realm of cognitive processes to develop strategies that effectively handle the fluid dynamics of negotiation. Harness these cognitive tools to navigate through negotiation scenarios, not just as transactions, but as conversations threaded with hidden psychological undercurrents. They orchestrate the rhythm of negotiation success.

Chapter 5. Planning and Preparing: The Bedrock of Negotiation

Good negotiation starts with preparation and planning. This fundamental backbone of negotiation provides a stable platform from which to explore, examine, and execute your negotiation strategies and techniques. Proper planning can determine the trajectory of your negotiation, align your goals, ensure your readiness to respond to various counter-arguments, and ultimately lead to more successful negotiation outcomes. Let's delve into the intricacies of planning and preparing by exploring sub-topics such as 'Doing Your Homework', 'Establishing Goals and Priorities', 'Anticipating the Other Party's Interests and Strategies', and 'Preparing a Meeting Agenda'.

5.1. Doing Your Homework

The first step in planning and preparing for negotiation is completing a thorough and meticulous investigation right at the initial stage, often referred to as 'Doing Your Homework'. This would involve researching all necessary information about your bargaining counterpart - their strengths and weaknesses, strategic orientations, past negotiation behavior and outcomes, market position, financial health, cultural background, etc. Such in-depth knowledge can provide necessary leverage in the negotiation process. You can utilise resources ranging from the corporation's official websites, annual reports, press releases to industrial analyses, market reports, and even social media to accumulate relevant information.

A crucial component of this 'homework' is also building a granular understanding of the negotiation issue in question. This encompasses both the tangible aspects like statistics, figures, market trends and intangible aspects including social implications, human elements and possible future scenarios.

5.2. Establishing Goals and Priorities

Once a comprehensive research has been conducted, the next step is establishing clear goals and prioritizing them. These goals should be a blend of both your organization's strategic objectives and personal aspirations in-line with the negotiation. It's essential to earmark both the 'ideal outcomes' and 'acceptable outcomes', akin to the negotiation's upper and lower limits.

Furthermore, assigning priorities can help streamline your negotiation strategy. This could range on a spectrum from 'non-negotiable' to 'could live without', allowing you to focus on what's genuinely essential and be flexible on other points. Conducting a SWOT (Strengths, Weaknesses, Opportunities, Threats) analysis on your position can help formulate these inputs effectively.

5.3. Anticipating the Other Party's Interests and Strategies

A successful negotiation doesn't stop at understanding your position, goals and strategies. It extends into empathetic understanding and anticipation of your counterpart's interests. This essentially means exploring the landscape from your counterpart's shoes, inferring their goals, aspirations, fears and strategies. Crafting 'what-if' scenarios based on their possible negotiation directions adds an additional layer of preparedness.

Equipped with such information, you can plot effective counter-strategies or propose alternatives that can align both parties' interests, laying down the path for a 'win-win' solution. This tactic is also productive in building trust which can result in longer-term cooperation.

5.4. Preparing a Meeting Agenda

The last step involves preparing a well-structured meeting agenda. It should list the discussion topics, their sequence, and possible durations. It's advisable to start with less controversial items to build an atmosphere of agreement and mutual understanding before heading onto more contentious issues.

Through this, it becomes easier to control the conversation's flow, ensuring important points are discussed and the negotiation remains focused and goal-oriented. However, such a rigid template should be flexible, leaving room for adjustments based on how the negotiation unfolds.

Preparation and planning are much like the unseen roots of a tree that nourish and facilitate the visible growth above the ground. Aptly understanding the nuances of these back-end processes will consequently reflect in the frontline negotiation performance.

In conclusion, the essence of negotiation lies not just in the dialogue that ensues, but the groundwork you've put in setting up the stage. Preparation forms the bedrock on which negotiation structures are built, playing a pivotal role in defining the negotiation direction and its eventual outcomes. This old saying perfectly sums this up, "By failing to prepare, you are preparing to fail." Let this serve as a reminder of the immense significance our preparation holds in the grand theater of negotiation.

Chapter 6. Effective Communication in Negotiation: Listening, Questioning, and Body Language

In the grand landscape of negotiations, communication plays a pivotal role not just in how we negotiate, but also in the outcomes that we are able to achieve. Three fundamental aspects of communication are critical to the successful conclusion of any negotiation: listening, questioning, and body language. This chapter offers an exhaustive exploration of these facets, replete with numerous practical tips and strategies to empower you to navigate the negotiation landscape with greater ease and assurance.

6.1. The Power of Listening in Negotiation

Listening is a key skill in any negotiation. It signals respect for the other party and lends itself to a more in-depth understanding of their perspectives. In turn, this can provide a crucial basis for identifying commonalities and bridging gaps in negotiation. Active listening goes beyond just hearing words to engaging with their deeper meaning and implications. This often involves acknowledging the speaker's sentiments, seeking clarification if things are unclear, and reframing or paraphrasing the content relayed to affirm understanding.

Remember, effective listening also entails discouraging interruptions and distractions while someone else is speaking. This level of attentiveness can promote trust and rapport building - both vital ingredients in successful negotiations. Moreover, keen listening may facilitate the identification of underlying issues or interests that may not have been explicitly communicated, thereby allowing you to address the real matter at hand.

6.2. Harnessing Questions in Negotiation

Questions, when wielded wisely, can be extraordinary tools in negotiation. They can facilitate information gathering, steer discussions in a preferred direction, challenge assumptions, clarify understanding, and even manage and diffuse confrontation. The type of questions used can also greatly influence negotiation dynamics. Open-ended questions, for instance, can solicit expansive responses, exploring the opponent's needs, priorities, or constraints, while closed-ended questions can help to confirm details or reach an agreement.

Strategic use of probing, solution-oriented, hypothetical, or mirror questions can further intensify engagement. One tactic to avoid, however, is using loaded questions, which emanate from assumptions and can lead to distortion of the truth or provoke hostility. By thoughtfully designing and deploying questions, a negotiator can create a conducive and collaborative atmosphere, encourage open dialogue, and progress towards mutually beneficial resolutions.

6.3. Decoding Body Language in Negotiation

Despite verbal interactions being central to any negotiation, non-verbal cues, or body language, play a critical role in shaping the negotiation space. Body language can either validate the verbal messages or contradict them, leading to perceived inauthenticity. This can include facial expressions, gestures, postures, proximity, eye contact, touch, and even paralinguistic cues such as voice tone, pace, volume, and inflections.

For instance, maintaining steady eye contact reflects confidence, sincerity and engagement while folded arms could signal defensiveness or resistance. Physical proximity and touch may denote varying degrees of comfort, trust or dominance, subject to cultural sensitivities. Similarly, adopting an open posture conveys approachability and willingness to collaborate, while an aggressive or dominant physical stance may escalate tension, potentially hindering the negotiation process.

A primary advantage of focusing on body language is that it can provide insights into the emotional state and true intentions of your negotiation partner, even when these are not verbally communicated. This can offer paths to further probe, pacify, or persuade the other party. However, accuracy in interpretation is crucial, as misreading non-verbal signals could lead to misunderstanding or conflict.

To gain the most from this insight into listening, questioning and body language, it's crucial to remember that these skills are interrelated and most effective when used in synchronicity. Employing them tactically, adapting to shifting dynamics, and acknowledging their potential can aid in shaping the negotiation trajectory towards your desired goals. In the subsequent sections, the emphasis will shift to bargaining strategies and techniques, building on the strong communicative foundation established in this section.

Chapter 7. Bargaining Strategies and Techniques

Bargaining is the heart of any negotiation, where the abstract art of influencing others meets the concrete world of prices, quantities, deadlines, and details. Nevertheless, effective bargaining is not about haggling, bluffing, or applying psychological pressure. Instead, it's a strategic exercise that hinges upon understanding the other party's interests, anticipating their responses, and crafting mutually beneficial solutions.

7.1. The Bargaining Spectrum

In a broad perspective, bargaining can be viewed as a spectrum with two fundamental strategies at its extremes - distributive bargaining, often referred to as 'win-lose,' and integrative bargaining, also known as 'win-win.' Understanding the mechanics of both is vital for selecting the most suitable technique for each negotiation scenario.

Distributive bargaining works on the premise of a fixed pie, where any gain for one party implies a loss for the other. Here, the focus is on maximizing personal benefit, often at the expense of the relationship with your counterpart. Though this approach might be suitable in one-off transactions where relationships are not a factor, the 'winner takes it all' philosophy might not work favorably in the long run.

On the other end of the spectrum, integrative bargaining centers on expanding the pie rather than fighting over existing pieces. It's based on the premise that each side has multiple interests, some of which may overlap, paving the way for creative solutions that satisfy both sets of interests. As a result, integrative bargaining is highly conducive to forming and strengthening relationships, making it an ideal strategy for long term and recurring negotiations.

7.2. Key Techniques for Effective Bargaining

Irrespective of the bargaining strategy you adopt, there are several universal techniques that can enhance your bargaining prowess:

BATNA (Best Alternative To a Negotiated Agreement): Always have a clear understanding of your BATNA. It's a powerful tool that sets a benchmark below which you should walk away from the proposed agreement. Not only does it prevent you from accepting unfavorable deals, but also it fortifies your bargaining position.

Anchoring: An initial offer (provided it's within a reasonable range) can 'anchor' the negotiations and shape both parties' expectations. Thus, if you have good reason or high confidence, don't shy away from making the first proposal.

Framing: Frame proposals in terms of gains rather than losses and borrow the language of your counterparts to enhance understanding and appeal.

Silence: Silence can put the pressure on the other party to bridge the expectant silence with concessions. But, it's wise to use this tool judiciously.

Concession Making: Concessions are powerful tools both for moving towards agreement and also for signaling cooperation. Make sure that your concessions are reciprocal, as giving without receiving erodes your bargaining power.

Decoy and Sunk Cost: Decoy is a negotiation technique where an unattractive offer is presented in conjunction with a more attractive offer, making the latter seem more valuable. Meanwhile, the sunk cost fallacy can be used to encourage sticking to a course once an investment — monetary, time, or effort — has been made.

7.3. Handling Tough Bargaining Tactics

Despite your best intentions, you might encounter negotiators who use aggressive or underhanded tactics. Some classic aggressive tactics include the 'exploding offer,' where an attractive deal is given an unnaturally short deadline, or the 'nibble,' where just as the deal is about to be inked, the other side adds a small request. When you encounter such strategies, be firm and unyielding, but avoid direct confrontation.

Among manipulative tactics, 'bogey' is a ploy used to pretend a minor issue is major. 'Chicken' involves risky or even outrageous behavior to force a concession. With these, it is important to question the justification and judge the other party's commitment fulfillment.

Moreover, be aware of 'power games,' where the negotiator might exert power by keeping you waiting, disrupting the meeting, or bringing a "higher authority" who is ideally hard to please. Keeping your cool and aiming for a professional conversation can negate their effects.

Lastly, remember to avoid personalizing the negotiation, engaging in arguments, or resorting to negative tactics yourself. Always maintain the high ground, stay professional, and focus on the mutual benefits of a successful negotiation.

7.4. Action Points

Bargaining is a delicate dance between interests, expectations, relationships, and results. It's much more than the exchange of offers and counter-offers. Consider the techniques discussed here as your tools just like a craftsman might use his tools to create a masterpiece. Practice them, adapt them, and use them to shape negotiations that lead to superior outcomes, fortified relationships, and opportunities for future cooperation.

With the right bargaining strategies and techniques in your portfolio, you are now ready to navigate the challenging waters of negotiation with increased confidence and competence, turning every discussion into a potential win-win outcome.

Chapter 8. Dealing with Difficult Negotiation Scenarios

Life presents us with a diverse range of negotiation scenarios, many of which are straightforward and amicable. Yet, there will inevitably be situations poised on the finer edge of complexity and fraught with conflict. These difficult negotiation scenarios pose unique challenges but also provide opportunities to display advanced negotiation prowess. The focus of this chapter is to guide you through the complexities of such scenarios, fortifying you with strategies to navigate them, and empowering you to turn potential conflict into productive dialogue and desirable outcomes.

8.1. Understanding Difficult Negotiation Scenarios

Difficult negotiation scenarios encompass a wide range of situations; from high-stake business deals, to resolving contentious disputes among parties holding diametrically opposed viewpoints and interests. They are often marked by high levels of emotional stress, conflict, unpredictability, and the potential for damaging long-term relationships- should they be managed poorly.

It is crucial to understand the nature of these challenging situations and why they are considered difficult. The factors that induce difficulty in negotiation can be diverse: vested interests, ambiguity in objectives, or high-pressure timelines, an absence of trust or mutual respect, power imbalances, and cultural or personal differences. The key to successfully managing challenging negotiation scenarios lies in understanding their intricacies, addressing them objectively and systematically, and employing specific strategies to overcome or leverage them effectively.

8.2. Embracing Conflict as an Opportunity

The first step in handling tough negotiation scenarios is to re-frame your perspective of conflict. Rather than perceiving it as a negative or a roadblock, embrace it as an opportunity for creative problem-solving. Conflict often exposes the need for change or the existence of dilemmas that require solutions. Adopting a positive frame of mind can ignite your innovative capabilities, allowing you to view stalemates as puzzles waiting to be solved. It's through these high-pressure situations that you can truly showcase your negotiation skills and temperament, leading to potential breakthroughs and robust agreements.

8.3. Strategising for Difficult Scenarios

Strategic planning for challenging negotiation scenarios involves several critical elements:

1. Establish Clear Goals: Articulate your objectives tightly and anticipate potential challenges that might hinder your path. Clarifying your goals can set the tone for the dialogue and help you stay focused when tension escalates.

2. Research and Understand Your Counterpart: Invest time to understand the other party's perspectives, interests, constraints, and communication style. This will help to foster empathy and illuminate new avenues for compromise.

3. Map Possible Outcomes: Create a comprehensive list of possible outcomes. This includes your Best Alternative to a Negotiated Agreement (BATNA), the Worst Alternative to a Negotiated

Agreement (WATNA), and the Zone of Possible Agreement (ZOPA). Having this foresight helps you manage expectations and gauge the progress of the negotiation.

4. Develop a Tactical Plan: Devise tactical responses to potential obstacles. These include indirections, a switch of topics, personal attacks, stonewalling, or positional bargaining.

8.4. Employing Powerful Negotiation Techniques

Once the strategic foundation is in place, apply technical acumen to push through the complexities. Powerful negotiation techniques will vary according to the situation, and may include the following:

1. Promoting Open Dialogue: Encourage all parties to communicate their concerns and interests openly. This will help you uncover hidden issues and gain valuable insights.

2. Leveraging Active Listening: This goes beyond merely hearing the words of the other party. It involves understanding their intrinsic message, including unspoken feelings, needs, or reservations.

3. Engaging in Joint Problem-Solving: Propose a collaborative approach to finding mutually beneficial solutions. Present your proposals as opportunities for joint gain rather than as individual victories.

4. Practicing Patience and Persistence: Difficult negotiations often require more time and patience. Practice persistence, resist the urge to rush, and give the process the time it needs.

8.5. Navigating through Impasses

Impasses or deadlocks can often appear in difficult negotiation scenarios. However, you can adopt certain tactics to break these deadlocks:

1. Changing the Environment: A shift in the environment, like a change of location, can provide a fresh perspective.

2. Introducing a Third Party: A neutral mediator can help facilitate dialogue and work towards a resolution.

3. Taking a Break: Taking time away can help diffuse tension and provide an opportunity for parties to re-evaluate their positions.

4. Segmenting or Bundling Issues: Depending on the situation, breaking down, or grouping issues together can help parties find points of agreement.

5. Exploring Concessions: Temporarily giving up on minor points can help to keep the negotiation in motion.

In conclusion, one must remember that even the most daunting negotiation scenarios present unique opportunities for growth and skill-enhancement. With resilience, strategic planning, and the ability to employ effective techniques, you have the power to transform difficult negotiation scenarios into extraordinary accomplishments. This approach ensures that the final outcome is not a one-off win or loss but the establishment of a sustainable, productive, and long-lasting negotiation relationship. Remember, every challenge faced is a potential victory waiting to be achieved. So, embrace the complexities of the negotiation process and stride forward with confidence and gallantry. Your negotiation journey is bound to be punctuated with moments of triumph, and this is what makes the journey all the more exhilarating and rewarding.

Chapter 9. Negotiating Across Cultures: Embracing Diversity and Differences

In an increasingly interconnected global environment, the skill to negotiate across cultural barriers stands out as a defining feature of a successful negotiator. The ability to recognize, understand, and suitably adapt to these diversified backgrounds can easily mean the difference between a smooth, successful negotiation and a disrupted, failed one. This chapter aims to impart the reader with that vital understanding and the necessary skills required to negotiate successfully in multicultural contexts.

9.1. Navigating Cultural Differences

Cultural dissimilarities pose unique challenges on the negotiation table. Such challenges include differences in communication styles, decision-making procedures, power dynamics, uncertainty tolerances, and definitions of time. The appreciation of these distinctions assumes significant importance in negotiating effectively. One must strive to acquire a cultural intelligence that overcomes potential misunderstandings or misinterpretations and leads to the forging of effective international relationships.

9.2. Understanding and Respecting Cultural Perspectives

Respect for other cultures is non-negotiable. It serves as an essential precursor to any successful cross-cultural negotiation. Always approach a new culture with openness, acknowledging that their customs and traditions, though different, are equally significant as yours. Acknowledge these diversities while maintaining focus on the negotiation goal. You should aim to create a balance where cultural sensitivity doesn't encourage bias or influence decision-making, yet is not disregarded.

9.3. Cross-Cultural Communication Styles

Effective communication serves as the backbone of successful negotiations. However, communication becomes more complex when different languages and cultural norms are involved. Every culture embodies unique nuances in their verbal and non-verbal communication, right from the use of silence, the volume and pitch of speech, to eye contact, body language, and physical touch. Awareness and sensitivity to such differences are indispensable in painting a comprehensive understanding of the other party's intentions.

9.4. Decision-Making Across Cultures

Ranging from collective decision-making witnessed in cultures valuing community consensus, to the individualistic approach seen in cultures placing emphasis on personal independence, the variance in decision-making procedures can be vast. Understanding these patterns can help shape your negotiation strategy. Recognizing how the final decision will be reached enables you to tailor your strategy to ensure your proposal is given due consideration.

9.5. The Role of Power and Hierarchy

Power dynamics and hierarchies vary significantly across cultures. Some cultures place high importance on status and may primarily engage their seniors in negotiation, while others opt for a democratic approach, involving all levels of personnel. Recognizing these differences and interacting appropriately with each member of the negotiating party fosters mutual respect, creating a favorable climate for negotiation.

9.6. Managing Uncertainty

Every culture has its unique level of discomfort with uncertainty, which affects how negotiators respond to situations where the outcomes are ambiguous. Some cultures may approach ambiguity with caution, while others may view it as an opportunity. Understanding these attitudes can help adapt your negotiation strategy to minimize anxiety and enhance collaboration.

9.7. Time Sensitivity Across Cultures

The perception of time varies considerably across cultures. In some cultures, time is viewed linearly, where punctuality and deadlines are highly regarded. In contrast, other cultures perceive time in a more fluid manner, viewing the relationship building during negotiation as more important than rigid timelines. Respecting these time perspectives can greatly smooth negotiation dynamics.

9.8. From Awareness to Application: Developing Strategies

It is of paramount importance that cultural awareness moves beyond mere theoretical understanding, converting into practical strategic adoption. Various strategies like active listening, asking questions sensitively, displaying respect, and employing patience can greatly assist in effective negotiation across cultures.

9.9. Case Studies: Successes and Failures

Compiling real-life examples, this section delves into instances where cross-cultural negotiations have flourished due to cultural intelligence or floundered due to its lack. Each case study encapsulates important lessons to be learned, providing an opportunity for the reader to reflect and learn from practical scenarios.

9.10. Beyond the Negotiation Table

The negotiation doesn't end with just signing the deal; it must go beyond to nurturing the relationship fostered through the negotiating process. This includes managing any post-negotiation conflicts, keeping lines of communication open, and maintaining a respectful relationship with the counterparts. Ultimately, cross-cultural negotiations are about promoting healthy business relationships globally. This chapter ends with a parting reminder that respect and understanding of cultural differences can direct all discussions towards a successful end.

In conclusion, negotiating across cultures necessitates tolerance, adaptability, and respect for diversity. The power to embrace these differences can empower you significantly in the international arena, enabling you to attain negotiated outcomes that satisfy all parties involved.

Chapter 10. From Theory to Practice: Real Life Case Studies

The path from abstract theory to tangible practice often seems dense, labyrinthine and difficult to navigate. Yet, the need to apply negotiation theories and strategies becomes crystal clear when we delve into real-life scenarios. It's in these real-world experiences that theoretical models, techniques, and strategies encounter complexities and challenges that are often obscured in the sterile, controlled environment of a classroom or textbook. Drawing from the fountains of various disciplines – be it psychology, sociology, economics or communications – this exploration aims to immerse you in the vivid arenas of negotiation, shedding light on the intricate, dynamic dance between theory and practice.

10.1. The Inevitable: Blend of Theoretical and Practical Approaches

Understanding the art of negotiation isn't merely an intellectual exercise; it's a well-rounded amalgamation of diverse strategies, theories, and practical applications. Think of theory as a roadmap providing you with an overall picture, a lay of the land, if you will. However, this roadmap isn't one-size-fits-all. It is continually subject to revision and reevaluation, as it confronts the unpredictable terrains of reality. One can cram all the negotiation theories, shake hands with numerous bargaining tactics, and yet find themselves gasping for air when thrown into the deep end of the real-life negotiation pool. Hence, the dire need for practical training that helps to integrate theory into experiences that challenge, stimulate and mold.

Case studies are compelling tools to bridge this gap. They present you with scenarios tailor-made to demonstrate the application of negotiation theories you've learned thus far. When scrutinizing a case, seek to spot the negotiation techniques employed, identify key elements that contributed to the outcomes, and ponder upon alternative strategies that might have been used. You're essentially navigating through an immersive labyrinth of negotiations, encountering real-life complexities, testing your theories, and refining your approaches.

10.2. Case Study Dissection: An exercise in Judicious Evaluation

Let's delve into our first case study revolving around a business negotiation scenario. In this instance, a reputed car dealer ('Dealer') is negotiating with a potential customer ('Customer'). The crux of the negotiation is the price of a luxury sedan. The Customer is aware that the Dealer often strays from the sticker price for serious buyers. Additionally, for the Dealer, maintaining customer satisfaction is crucial to ensure repeat business.

Read between the lines of this scenario, and you'd identify the principal theory at play: the integrative negotiation model. The Dealer and the Customer's interests are multi-dimensional. The Dealer seeks to sell at a higher rate while also nurturing a relationship conducive for future business. Similarly, the Customer craves satisfactory purchase price, as well ensuring his status as a valued patron.

Analyzing this case, dissect how different tactics could lead towards these outcomes. What if the Customer decided to co-opt the tactic of anchoring by stating a lower price upfront? Or suppose the Dealer leveraged the research theory, unconcealing the customer's car preferences through a friendly chat, effectively targeting the customer's needs? Dissect these possibilities and more while remembering that there might be several correct ways to address a negotiation, depending on the parties and their interests.

10.3. Eliciting Lessons: Mining Nuggets of Wisdom

Shifting the gear, let's explore a second case study derived from a classic environmental negotiation scenario. A coastal region, infamous for its hazardous waste issues fueled by a local industry, witnesses an innovative negotiation between the local community, environmentalists, the industry and the local government. The environmentalists desire stringent regulations on the industry, the industry seeks continued operation without hefty fines, the local community yearns for a detoxified environment, and the local government desires to satisfy its constituents while promoting the area's economic growth.

Navigating the gloriously messy and multi-stakeholder nature of the case, the negotiation arena resonates with lessons on collaboration, coalition forming, mutually beneficial solutions, and empathetic understanding. Submerge yourself into these waters, exploring how negotiation tactics play into the real-world scenario. What if the industry proposed a long-term cleanup initiative, which could appease the environmentalists and also demonstrate their commitment to community welfare? What if the local government analyzed the scenario from a BATNA (Best Alternative to a Negotiated Agreement) and WATNA (Worst Alternative to a Negotiated Agreement) perspective, orchestrating a collective negotiation strategy to simultaneously achieve economic growth and environmental detoxification?

10.4. Conclusion: The Grand Finale

The voyage from abstract negotiation theories to the vibrant tapestry of real-world negotiations is a fascinating one, scattered with both challenges and treasures. Absorb the lessons these case studies offer and explore the plethora of others available, each providing fresh insights, perspectives and opportunities for growth. Equipped with practical knowledge coupled with theoretical underpinnings, march forth into the provocative world of negotiation, transforming conversations into triumphs and discord into harmony. This mixture of theory and practice in negotiation isn't just an art; it is a symphony, each note contributing to the masterpiece. With each real-life negotiation you encounter, you're both the conductor and the performer, steering the symphony whilst dancing to its tune.

Featured case studies do not cover all negotiation scenarios a reader might face but worry not; they are but brief samples in a vast smorgasbord! Strive to encourage your curiosity, analyze more case studies, partake in simulations and roll play activities to learn, unlearn and relearn. Find joy in this ongoing process and remember that while victorious negotiations may feel breathtaking, it's the journey that shapes a negotiator. The magical realm of negotiation where theory meets practice beckons! Step forth and transform every conversation into a vibrant dance of persuasion, compromise, collaboration, and success!

Chapter 11. Closing the Deal and Beyond: Negotiation Follow-up

As we approach the culmination of our deep exploration into the labyrinth of negotiation, let us delve into the final stage, meticulously exploring the art of closing the deal and, crucially, the following elaboration of a negotiation follow-up mechanism. The realm of negotiation does not conclude with the final agreement; just as important is the intricate dance of maintaining the agreement's legitimacy, uncovering the seeds of future opportunities, and nurturing the relationship established during the negotiation process.

11.1. The Final Stretch: Perfecting Agreement Closure Techniques

Your exhaustive preparation, acute understanding of negotiation psychology, effective communication skills, and agile maneuvering through negotiation scenarios has brought you to the final stage -concluding the negotiation. This is the moment to confirm the hard-fought gains of your negotiation process and to ensure all parties involved are content with the results. It is crucial to leave no stone unturned, for even a seemingly perfect negotiation may crumble if the closure strategies are erroneous.

The first point to ensure is that all terms, conditions, and expectations are clarified and accepted by all parties involved. This can eliminate potential discrepancies and misunderstandings in the future. If possible, put everything in writing. It serves both as a reminder of the agreed terms and a legally valid document evidencing the negotiation outcome. Time could be of the essence, so ensure the deal closure doesn't drag on unnecessarily. Lastly, appreciate and acknowledge the efforts of all parties, framing the negotiation as a win-win rather than a zero-sum game.

11.2. Sowing the Seeds: Post-Negotiation Establishments

Following the closure of a negotiation, the task at hand involves instituting specific post-negotiation mechanisms. These serve multiple purposes, such as validation of agreement terms, early detection of potential conflicts, performance tracking, and future negotiation groundwork. The first step post-negotiation involves revisiting and scrutinizing the negotiation proceedings. Create a post-mortem report detailing crucial turning points, strategies employed, the reaction of the other party, outcomes, etc. This serves as a treasure trove of information for future negotiations, enabling lessons learned to be put to good use.

Regular follow-ups with the other party or parties involved can also be instrumental in maintaining the momentum of the agreement and smoothening out any operational kinks. Performance tracking and early conflict detection mechanisms can help in identifying deviations from the agreed path and enable prompt corrective action. Avenues for dispute resolution must also be accounted for in order to prevent potential disputes from snowballing into major conflicts.

11.3. Fostering Relationship: Towards Future Opportunities

Just as in everyday life, in the world of negotiation too, maintaining a healthy professional relationship even post the negotiation process holds immense value. Illustrating appreciation for the other party's cooperation, sharing constructive feedback, congratulating upon successful milestones, and expressing a desire to work again in the future strengthens the bond between the negotiating parties. It ensures not only better adherence to the negotiated agreement but also opens the door to future negotiation and collaboration opportunities.

Nurture the established relationship, not as a transactional necessity but as the cultivation of a fruitful partnership for the future. This aspect is often overlooked in the negotiation process, where the focus lies more on 'gaining the most.' But as you steer towards protracted negotiation horizons, you will find that this relationship building aspect often turns the tide in your favor.

This report has guided you through the vast maze of negotiation, shedding light upon its strategic turning points, psychological undertones, and crucial preparation aspects. As we draw to a close, it is crucial to remember the cyclical nature of negotiation. It never truly ends. Every close leads to the start of a follow-up, every follow-up paves the way for future negotiations. The art of negotiation is ever-evolving and deeply layered, and the more you immerse yourself, the more proficient you become. Embrace the perpetual journey, savor the successes, learn from the setbacks, and venture forth with a newfound sense of confidence and insight.

www.ingramcontent.com/pod-product-compliance
Lightning Source LLC
Chambersburg PA
CBHW070140230526
45472CB00004B/1613